ON CHRISTIAN

ARIEL BOOKS

ANDREWS AND McMEEL
KANSAS CITY

ISBN: 0-8362-0720-3

Library of Congress Catalog Card Number: 95-76438

INTRODUCTION

What does it mean to be Christian? Most of us are good people. We teach our children the values our parents taught us . . . to share our things, to be kind to others, and to say our prayers at night. Some of us need a little more encouragement and, perhaps, proof. "Okay, God," we may bargain, "if you're really up there, help me find my lost wallet." Then the telephone rings and some kind soul has called to say that he found your wallet in a restaurant. He returns it—with all your money still in it. "It's a miracle!" you exclaim and vow to make it to church next Sunday.

But Christianity is not just about asking God for things and expecting miracles. It's not just something to turn to when we're in dire straits. Christianity is a way of living. It's loving your neighbor, even though you're sure he dumps his leaves on your side of the fence. It's being faithful to your spouse, your family, and your friends. It's forgiving those who have wronged you; it's expressing gratitude, repentance, faith, and joy. Most important, it's about love . . . and that's what this book and the Christian life are all about. ☩

I shall pass through this world but once. If therefore there be any kindness I can show, or any good thing I can do, let me do it now; let me not defer it or neglect it.

✠ ÉTIENNE DE GRELLET ✠

(ATTRIBUTED)

There is no surprise more magical than the surprise of being loved: it is God's finger on man's shoulder.

CHARLES MORGAN

It is not how much we have, but how much we enjoy, that makes happiness.

CHARLES HADDON SPURGEON

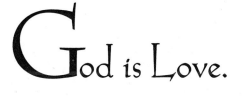

God is Love.

✠

MARY BAKER EDDY

It is a great deal better to live a holy life than to talk about it. Lighthouses do not ring bells and fire cannons to call attention to their shining—they just shine.

✣ DWIGHT L. MOODY ✣

The Infinite
Goodness has such
wide arms that it takes
whatever turns to it.

✠

DANTE

For the poor shall never cease out of the land: therefore I command thee, saying, Thou shalt open thine hand wide unto thy brother, to thy poor, and to thy needy, in thy land.

✝ DEUTERONOMY 15:11 ✝

He who thinks most of heaven will do most for earth.

ANONYMOUS

15

Where your pleasure is, there is your treasure: where your treasure, there your heart; where your heart, there your happiness.

ST. AUGUSTINE

I maintain
Christianity is a life
much more than a
religion.

R. M. MOBERLY

Peace is not just the absence of war . . . Like a cathedral, peace must be constructed patiently and with unshakable faith.

✠ POPE JOHN PAUL II ✠

Little deeds of kindness, little
words of love,
Help to make earth happy like
the heaven above.

Julia A. Fletcher Carney

For what is a man advantaged, if he gain the whole world, and lose himself, or be cast away?

✛ LUKE 9:25 ✛

May the road rise to meet you.
May the wind be ever at your back.
May the Good Lord keep you in the hollow
  of His hand.
May your heart be as warm as your hearthstone.
And when you come to die
may the wail of the poor be the only sorrow
you'll leave behind.
May God bless you always.

ANONYMOUS

Prayer is a strong wall and fortress of the church; it is a goodly Christian's weapon.

✠ MARTIN LUTHER ✠

For we brought nothing into this world, and it is certain we can carry nothing out.

✝ I TIMOTHY 6:7 ✝

Not what we give, but what we share,—
For the gift without the giver is bare;
Who gives himself with his alms feeds three—
Himself, his hungering neighbor, and me.

✠ JAMES RUSSELL LOWELL ✠

24

Hope is wanting something so eagerly that—in spite of all the evidence that you're not going to get it—you go right on wanting it.

✠ NORMAN VINCENT PEALE ✠

If you wish to be brothers, let the arms fall from your hands. One cannot love while holding offensive arms.

✠ POPE PIUS VI ✠

Never forget that [God] tests his real friends more severely than the lukewarm ones.

✚ KATHRYN HULME ✚

Hope springs eternal
in the human breast:
Man never is,
but always to be blest.

✠ ALEXANDER POPE ✠

Faith is a living and
unshakeable confidence, a belief
in the grace of God so assured
that a man would die a thousand
deaths for its sake.

✠ MARTIN LUTHER ✠

If a friend is in trouble, don't annoy him by asking if there is anything you can do. Think up something appropriate and do it.

✛ EDGAR WATSON HOWE ✛

A holy life is not an ascetic, or gloomy, or solitary life, but a life regulated by divine truth and faithful in Christian duty.—It is living above the world while we are still in it.

✠ TRYON EDWARDS ✠

In the act of worship itself, the experience of liberation becomes a constituent of the community's being ... It is the power of God's Spirit invading the lives of the people, "buildin' them up where they are torn down and proppin' them up on every leanin' side."

JAMES H. CONE

He that saith he is in the light, and hateth his brother, is in darkness even until now.

✣ I JOHN 2:9 ✣

It is the great work of nature to transmute sunlight into life. So it is the great end of Christian living to transmute the light of truth into the fruits of holy living.

✝ ADONIRAM J. GORDON ✝

I have learned that human existence is essentially tragic. It is only the love of God, disclosed and enacted in Christ, that redeems the human tragedy and makes it tolerable. No, more than tolerable. Wonderful.

BISHOP ANGUS DUN

For Mercy has a human heart,
Pity, a human face,
And Love, the human form divine,
And Peace, the human dress.

Then every man of every clime,
That prays in his distress,
Prays to the human form divine
Love Mercy Pity Peace.

WILLIAM BLAKE

Humility is strong—not bold; quiet—not speechless; sure—not arrogant.

✛ ESTELLE SMITH ✛

Forgiveness is not an occasional act; it is a permanent attitude.

MARTIN LUTHER KING, JR.

The Lord's Resurrection is not an isolated fact, it is a fact that concerns the whole of mankind; from Christ it extends to the world; it has a cosmic importance . . . the source of meaning of the human drama, the solution of the problem of evil, the origin of a new form of life, to which we give the name of Christianity.

POPE PAUL VI

You may have living and habitual conversation in heaven, under the aspect of the most simple, ordinary life. Remember that holiness does not consist in doing uncommon things, but in doing every thing with purity of heart.

CARDINAL HENRY E. MANNING

There is nothing so well
known as that we should not
expect something for nothing—
but we all do and call it Hope.

✦ EDGAR WATSON HOWE ✦

Hope arouses, as nothing else can arouse, a passion for the possible.

WILLIAM SLOANE COFFIN, JR.

To be like Christ is
to be a Christian.

WILLIAM PENN

The soul is the aspect of ourselves that is specific of our nature and distinguishes man from all other animals. We are not capable of defining this familiar and profoundly mysterious entity.

ALEXIS CARREL

Dost thou wish to receive mercy? Show mercy to thy neighbor.

ST. JOHN CHRYSOSTOM

Give strength, give thought, give deeds, give wealth;
Give love, give tears, and give thyself.
Give, give, be always giving.
Who gives not is not living;
The more you give, the more you live.

ANONYMOUS

We can do no great things; only small things with great love.

MOTHER TERESA

Once you accept the existence of God—
however you define him, however you explain
your relationship to him—then you are caught
forever with his presence in the center of all
things.

MORRIS WEST

My duty towards my neighbor is to love him as myself, and to do all men as I would they should do unto me.

✠ BOOK OF COMMON PRAYER ✠

Being religious means asking passionately the question of the meaning of our existence and being willing to receive answers, even if the answers hurt.

✛ PAUL TILLICH ✛

Between whom there is hearty truth, there is love.

HENRY DAVID THOREAU

He that is a good man, is three quarters of his way toward being a good Christian wheresoever he lives, or whatsoever he is called.

✠ ROBERT SOUTH ✠

Our country
is the world—our
countrymen
are all mankind.

WILLIAM LLOYD GARRISON

Christianity teaches that the human soul is directly related to God. Such immediacy is the hallmark of the Divinity of the soul and the center of our freedom.

✠ HELMUT KUHN ✠

Goodness consists not in the outward things we do, but in the inward thing we are.—To be good is the great thing.

✠ EDWIN HUBBELL CHAPIN ✠

Joy, shipmate, joy!
(Pleas'd to my soul at death I cry,)
Our life is closed, our life begins,
The long, long anchorage we leave,
The ship is clear at last, she leaps!
She swiftly courses from the shore,
Joy, shipmate, joy.

WALT WHITMAN

Honor thy father and thy mother, as the Lord thy God hath commanded thee; that thy days may be prolonged, and that it may go well with thee, in the land which the Lord thy God giveth thee.

DEUTERONOMY 5:16

Social justice cannot be
attained by violence. Violence
kills what it intends to create.

✠ POPE JOHN PAUL II ✠

Grace comes into the soul, as
the morning sun into the world;
first a dawning; then a light; and
at last the sun in his full and
excellent brightness.

✝ THOMAS ADAMS ✝

Christ does not save us by acting a parable of divine love; he acts the parable of divine love by saving us. That is the Christian faith.

✝ AUSTIN FARBER ✝

An honest man's the noblest work of God.

ALEXANDER POPE

Self-sacrifice is the real miracle out of which all the reported miracles grew.

RALPH WALDO EMERSON

Out of our beliefs are born deeds; out of our deeds we form habits; out of our habits grows our character; and on our character we build our destiny.

✣ HENRY HANCOCK ✣

W

e are not sent into this
world to do anything into which
we cannot put our hearts.

✠ JOHN RUSKIN ✠

When you have learned to believe in God's purpose for you as an individual, you are immediately lifted out of the mass and become significant and meaningful in the eyes of God and of man.

JOHN SUTHERLAND BONNELL

People don't come to church for preachments, of course, but to daydream about God.

✝ KURT VONNEGUT, JR. ✝

The Christian life that is joyless is a discredit to God and a disgrace to itself.

✟ MALTBIE D. BABCOCK ✟

Amazing grace! How sweet the sound
That saved a wretch like me!
I once was lost, but now am found,
Was blind, but now I see.

JOHN NEWTON

Real joy comes not from ease or riches or from the praise of men, but from doing something worthwhile.

✠ SIR WILFRED GRENFELL ✠

We are born believing. A man bears beliefs as a tree bears apples.

Rejoice in the Lord always: and again I say, Rejoice.

PHILIPPIANS 4:4

Occupation was one of the pleasures of Paradise, and we cannot be happy without it.

✛ ANNA BROWNELL JAMESON ✛

Because I could not stop for Death,
He kindly stopped for me—
The Carriage held but just Ourselves
And Immortality.

EMILY DICKINSON

Do you wish to be great? Then begin by being. Do you desire to construct a vast and lofty fabric? Think first about the foundation of humility. The higher your structure is to be, the deeper must be its foundation.

ST. AUGUSTINE

The more merciful
Acts thou dost, the
more Mercy thou wilt
receive.

WILLIAM PENN

75

Humbleness is always grace; always dignity.

JAMES RUSSELL LOWELL

Each of us has his gift. Let us not imagine that we are disinherited by our heavenly Father, any one of us. Let us be ourselves, as God made us, then we shall be something good and useful.

JAMES FREEMAN CLARKE

Forgiveness is the answer to the child's dream of a miracle by which what is broken is made whole again, what is soiled is again made clean.

✛ DAG HAMMARSKJÖLD ✛

No man will learn anything at all, Unless he first will learn humility.

OWEN MEREDITH

God is a Spirit: and they that worship him must worship him in spirit and in truth.

JOHN 4:24

If thou desire the love of God and man, be humble, for the proud heart, as it loves none but itself, is beloved of none but itself.—Humility enforces where neither virtue, nor strength, nor reason can prevail.

FRANCIS QUARLES

Lord, make me an instrument of Your peace. Where there is hatred let me sow love; where there is injury, pardon; where there is doubt, faith; where there is despair, hope; where there is darkness, light; and where there is sadness, joy.

O divine Master, grant that I may not so much seek to be consoled as to console; to be understood as to understand; to be loved as to love. For it is in giving that we receive; it is in pardoning that we are pardoned; and it is in dying that we are born to eternal life.

✠ SAINT FRANCIS OF ASSISI ✠

(ATTRIBUTED)

I

f you do not tell the truth about yourself you cannot tell it about other people.

VIRGINIA WOOLF

It is no great thing to be
humble when you are brought
low; but to be humble when you
are praised is a great and rare
attainment.

✠ ST. BERNARD OF CLAIRVAUX ✠

For the Son of man is come to save that which was lost.

MATTHEW 18:11

Make a rule, and pray to God to help you
to keep it, never, if possible, to lie down at
night without being able to say: "I have made
one human being at least a little wiser, or a little
happier, or at least a little better this day."

CHARLES KINGSLEY

Teach me good judgment and knowledge: for I have believed thy commandments.

✠ PSALMS 119:66 ✠

And I will show that there is no imperfection in the present, and can be none in the future,
And I will show that whatever happens to anybody it may be turn'd to beautiful results,
And I will show that nothing can happen more beautiful than death.

WALT WHITMAN

It is well to give when asked,
but it is better to give unasked,
through understanding.

✢ KAHLIL GIBRAN ✢

Neither genius, fame, nor love show the greatness of the soul. Only kindness can do that.

JEAN BAPTISTE HENRI LACORDAIRE

*S*ometimes I think
that just not thinking
of oneself is a form
of prayer . . .

BARBARA GRIZZUTI HARRISON

Gladness of the heart is the life of man, and the joyfulness of a man prolongeth his days.

ECCLESIASTICUS 30:22
THE APOCRYPHA

To err is human, to forgive, divine.

ALEXANDER POPE

*S*orrows remembered
sweeten present joy.

ROBERT POLLOK

Grant us a common faith that man shall know bread and peace—that he shall know justice and righteousness, freedom and security, an equal opportunity and an equal chance to do his best not only in our own lands, but throughout the world. And in that faith let us march toward the clean world our hands can make.

STEPHEN VINCENT BENÉT

Our todays make our tomorrows, and our present lives determine the bridge on which we must enter the next life.

✛ MINOT J. SAVAGE ✛

Confess your faults one to another, and pray one for another, that ye may be healed. The effectual fervent prayer of a righteous man availeth much.

✠ JAMES 5:16 ✠

Kind words are the music of the world. They have a power which seems to be beyond natural causes, as if they were some angel's song which had lost its way and come on earth. It seems as if they could almost do what in reality God alone can do—soften the hard and angry hearts of men. No one was ever corrected by a sarcasm—crushed, perhaps, if the sarcasm was clever enough, but drawn nearer to God, never.

✠ FREDERICK WILLIAM FABER ✠

I f it were not for hopes, the heart would break.

THOMAS FULLER

A Christian is nothing but a sinful man who has put himself to school for Christ for the honest purpose of becoming better.

✛ HENRY WARD BEECHER ✛

The truest end of life
is to know the life that
never ends.

WILLIAM PENN

At end of Love, at end of Life,
At end of Hope, at end of Strife,
At end of all we cling to so—
The sun is setting—we must go.
At dawn of Love, at dawn of Life,
At dawn of Peace that follows Strife,
At dawn of all we long for so—
The sun is rising—let us go.

LOUISE CHANDLER MOULTON

This is what Christianity is for—to teach men the art of Life. And its whole curriculum lies in one word, "Learn of me."

✛ ANONYMOUS ✛

I believe in Christianity as I believe that the sun has risen, not only because I see it but because I see everything in it.

✝ C. S. LEWIS ✝

Live as with God; and
whatever be your calling, pray
for the gift that will perfectly
qualify you in it.

✠ HORACE BUSHNELL ✠

In the faces of men and women I see God and in my own face in the glass, I find letters from God dropt in the street, and every one is signed by God's name, and I leave them where they are, for I know that wheresoever I go others will punctually come for ever and ever.

WALT WHITMAN

Be good, keep your feet dry, your eyes open, your heart at peace, and your soul in the joy of Christ.

✠ THOMAS MERTON ✠

Little self-denials, little honesties, little passing words of sympathy, little nameless acts of kindness, little silent victories over favorite temptations—these are the silent threads of gold which, when woven together, gleam out so brightly in the pattern of life that God approves.

FREDERIC WILLIAM FARRAR

The Lord is good, a strong hold in the day of trouble; and he knoweth them that trust in him.

✙ NAHUM 1:7 ✙

My soul is like a mirror in which the glory of God is reflected, but sin, however insignificant, covers the mirror with smoke.

✠ ST. THERESA ✠

The cross is the ladder to heaven.

THOMAS DRAXE

The great use of life
is to spend it for some—
thing that outlasts it.

WILLIAM JAMES

Prayer is essentially about
making the heart strong so that
fear cannot penetrate there.

✠ MATTHEW FOX ✠

Do not abandon yourselves
to despair . . . We are the Easter
people and hallelujah is our song.

✠ POPE JOHN PAUL II ✠

Not where I breathe, but where I love, I live.

Robert Southwell

I would not say I believe. I know! I have had the experience of being gripped by something that is stronger than myself, something that people call God.

✠ CARL JUNG ✠

A man does a lot of prayer in an enemy prison. Prayer, even more than sheer thought, is the firmest anchor.

✝ JEREMIAH A. DENTON, JR. ✝

Goodness is the only investment that never fails.

HENRY DAVID THOREAU

There is a comfort and a strength in love;
'Twill make a thing endurable, which else
Would overset the brain, or break the heart.

WILLIAM WORDSWORTH

Nothing we do, however virtuous, can be accomplished alone; therefore we are saved by love.

✠ REINHOLD NIEBUHR ✠

Sin is a state of mind, not an outward act.

WILLIAM SEWELL

I have not the courage to search through books for beautiful prayers . . . Unable either to say them all or choose between them, I do as a child would do who cannot read—I say just what I want to say to God, quite simply, and He never fails to understand.

ST. THÉRÈSE OF LISIEUX

A sinful heart
makes feeble hand.

SIR WALTER SCOTT

Come lovely and soothing death,
Undulate round the world, serenely arriving,
arriving,
In the day, in the night, to all, to each,
Sooner or later delicate death.

WALT WHITMAN

Christianity is one beggar telling another beggar where he found bread.

D. T. NILES

Sin has four characteristics: self-sufficiency instead of faith, self-will instead of submission, self-seeking instead of benevolence, self-righteousness instead of humility.

E. PAUL HOVEY

He that ruleth over men must be just, ruling in the fear of God. And he shall be as the light of the morning, when the sun riseth, even a morning without clouds; as the tender grass springing out of the earth be clear shining after rain.

II Samuel 23:3–4

*S*orrow is better than laughter: for by the sadness of the countenance the heart is made better.

✠ ECCLESIASTES 7:3 ✠

Mental prayer is nothing else . . . but being on terms of friendship with God, frequently conversing in secret with Him.

✛ ST. TERESA OF AVILA ✛

God is not a cosmic bellboy for whom we can press a button to get things done.

HARRY EMERSON FOSDICK

The soul would have
no rainbow had the
eye no tears.

JOHN VANCE CHENEY

We live by desire to live; we live by choice; by will, by thought, by virtue, by the vivacity of the laws which we obey, and obeying share their life,—or we die by sloth, by disobedience, by losing hold of life, which ebbs out of us.

RALPH WALDO EMERSON

I can see, and that is why I can be happy, in what you call the dark, but which to me is golden. I can see a God-made world, not a man-made world.

✛ HELEN KELLER ✛

Let love be genuine; hate what is evil, hold fast to what is good; love one another with brotherly affection; outdo one another in showing honor. Never flag in zeal, be aglow with the Spirit, serve the Lord. Rejoice in your hope, be patient in tribulation, be constant in prayer.

ROMANS 12:9–12

Hope is the thing with feathers
That perches in the soul,
And sings the tune without the words,
And never stops at all.

EMILY DICKINSON

Repentance is not
self-regarding, but God-regarding.
It is not self-loathing, but
God-loving.

✠ FULTON J. SHEEN ✠

To have faith where you cannot see; to be willing to work on in the dark; to be conscious of the fact that, so long as you strive for the best, there are better things on the way, this in itself is success.

KATHERINE LOGAN

I asked God for strength, that I might achieve
I was made weak, that I might learn humbly to obey . . .
I asked for health, that I might do greater things
I was given infirmity, that I might do better things . . .
I asked for riches, that I might be happy
I was given poverty, that I might be wise . . .
I asked for power, that I might have the praise of men
I was given weakness, that I might feel the need of God . . .
I asked for all things, that I might enjoy life
I was given life that I might enjoy all things . . .
I got nothing that I asked for—but everything I had
    hoped for
Almost despite myself, my unspoken prayers were answered.
I am, among all men, most richly blessed.

✠ ANONYMOUS ✠

The value of persistent prayer
is not that he will hear us . . . but
that we will finally hear him.

✜ WILLIAM McGILL ✜

The whole history of the Christian life is a series of resurrections ... Every time a man finds his heart is troubled, that he is not rejoicing in God, a resurrection must follow; a resurrection out of the night of troubled thought into the gladness of the truth.

GEORGE MACDONALD

Your success and happiness lie in you.
External conditions are the accidents of life.
The great enduring realities are love and service.
Joy is the holy fire that keeps our purpose warm
and our intelligence aglow. Resolve to keep
happy, and your joy and you shall form an
invincible host against difficulty.

HELEN KELLER

Love truth, but pardon error.

Voltaire

Joys are our wings, sorrows our spurs.

JEAN PAUL RICHTER

Jesus answered and said unto them, This is the work of God, that ye believe on him whom he hath sent.

✤ JOHN 6:29 ✤

The body, that is but dust; the soul, it is a bud of eternity.

NATHANAEL CULVERWEL

Love is a mutual
self-giving which
ends in self-recovery.

BISHOP FULTON J. SHEEN

To have grown
wise and kind is
real success.

ANONYMOUS

147

All things bright and beautiful,
All creatures great and small,
All things wise and wonderful,
The Lord God made them all.

CECIL FRANCES ALEXANDER

Through prayer we can carry in our heart all human pain and sorrow, all conflicts and agonies, all torture and war, all hunger, loneliness, and misery, not because of some great psychological or emotional capacity, but because God's heart has become one with ours.

HENRI NOUWEN

Teach me to feel
another's woe,
To hide the fault I see:
That mercy I to others show,
That mercy show to me.

✠ ALEXANDER POPE ✠

We should pray to the angels, for they are given to us as guardians.

ST. AMBROSE

Christian life
consists of faith and
charity.

MARTIN LUTHER

Next to love, sympathy is the divinest passion of the human heart.

EDMUND BURKE

The more we are afflicted in this world, the greater is our assurance for the next; the more we sorrow in the present, the greater will be our joy in the future.

✠ St. Isidore of Seville ✠

*S*uffering accepted and
vanquished . . . will give you a
serenity which may well prove the
most exquisite fruit of your life.

✠ CARDINAL MERCIER ✠

Believe all the good you can of everyone. Do not measure others by yourself. If they have advantages which you have not, let your liberality keep pace with their good fortune. Envy no one, and you need envy no one.

WILLIAM HAZLITT

Whoever is spared personal pain must feel himself called to help in diminishing the pain of others. We must all carry our share of the misery which lies upon the world.

ALBERT SCHWEITZER

God does not die on the day when we cease to believe in a personal deity, but we die on the day when our lives cease to be illuminated by the steady radiance, renewed daily, of a wonder, the source of which is beyond all reason.

DAG HAMMARSKJÖLD

Joy is a constituent of life, a necessity of life; it is an element of life's value and life's power. As every man has need of joy, so too, every man has a right to joy . . . It is a condition of religious living.

PAUL WILHELM VON KEPPLER

Life without thankfulness is devoid of love and passion. Hope without thankfulness is lacking in fine perception. Faith without thankfulness lacks strength and fortitude. Every virtue divorced from thankfulness is maimed and limps along the spiritual road.

JOHN HENRY JOWETT

Reason is an action of the mind; knowledge is a possession of the mind; but faith is an attitude of the person. It means you are prepared to stake yourself on something being so.

✠ MICHAEL RAMSEY ✠

It is a good thing to give thanks unto the Lord.

PSALMS 92:1

The perfection of the
Christian life principally
and essentially
consists in charity . . .
which in some sort unites
or joins man to his end.

✠ POPE JOHN XXII ✠

My reason
nourishes my faith
and my faith my
reason.

NORMAN COUSINS

Why comes temptation, but
for man to meet
And master and make crouch
beneath his foot,
And so be pedestaled in triumph?

✣ ROBERT BROWNING ✣

The good neighbor looks beyond the external accidents and discerns those inner qualities that make all men human and, therefore, brothers.

✠ MARTIN LUTHER KING, JR. ✠

The very contradictions in my life are in some ways signs of God's mercy to me.

✚ THOMAS MERTON ✚

Temptations, when we first meet them, are as the lion that roared upon Samson; but if we overcome them, the next time we see them we shall find a nest of honey within them.

JOHN BUNYAN

Fight the good fight of faith.

I Timothy 6:12

Every moment of resistance to temptation is a victory.

FREDERICK WILLIAM FABER

Be not afraid of life. Believe that life *is* worth living and your belief will help create the fact.

✠ WILLIAM JAMES ✠

Do today's duty, fight today's temptation; and do not weaken and distract yourself by looking forward to things which you cannot see, and could not understand if you saw them.

CHARLES KINGSLEY

I can do all things through Christ which strengtheneth me.

PHILIPPIANS 4:13

This coming to know Christ is what makes Christian truth redemptive truth, the truth that transforms, not just the truth that informs . . .

✠ HAROLD COOKE PHILLIPS ✠

It is only the souls that do not love that go empty in this world.

ROBERT HUGH BENSON

It is not the eye that sees the beauty of the heaven, nor the ear that hears the sweetness of music or the glad tidings of a prosperous occurrence, but the soul, that perceives all the relishes of sensual and intellectual perfections; and the more noble and excellent the soul is, the greater and more savory are its perceptions.

JEREMY TAYLOR

Be content with
such things as ye have.

HEBREWS 8:5

The finest test of character is seen in the amount and the power of gratitude we have.

✙ MILO H. GATES ✙

Where love is concerned, too much is not even enough.

PIERRE-AUGUSTIN DE BEAUMARCHAIS

For the Christian who loves God, worship is the daily bread of patience.

HONORÉ DE BALZAC

The eternal God is thy refuge, and underneath are the everlasting arms.

DEUTERONOMY 33:27

Do not forget that even as
"to work is to worship"
so to be cheery is to worship also,
and to be happy is the first step
to being pious.

✠ ROBERT LOUIS STEVENSON ✠

Let the burden be never so heavy, love makes it light.

ROBERT BURTON

Repentance is the heart's sorrow, and a clear life ensuing.

WILLIAM SHAKESPEARE

184

Set your affections
on things above, not
on things on the earth.

COLOSSIANS 3:2

The ship's place is in the sea, but God pity the ship when the sea gets into it. The Christian's place is in the world, but God pity the Christian if the world gets the best of him.

A new commandment I give unto you, that you love one another.

JOHN 13:34

187

Be ye therefore wise as serpents, and harmless as doves.

MATTHEW 10:16

None but a good man is really a living man, and the more good any man does, the more he really lives. All the rest is death, or belongs to it.

COTTON MATHER

Virtue is not to be considered in the light of mere innocence, or abstaining from harm; but as the exertion of our faculties in doing good.

JOSEPH BUTLER

The danger is not lest the soul should doubt whether there is any bread, but lest, by a lie, it should persuade itself that it is not hungry.

SIMONE WEIL

Obedience, judgment, witness . . . these are the signposts to our salvation, in all the perplexities and busyness of our life.

STEPHEN BAYNE

Of all duties, the love of truth, with faith and constancy in it, ranks first and highest. To love God and to love truth are one and the same.

✠ SILVIO PELLICO ✠

He who loves
brings God and the
world together.

MARTIN BUBER

Sunday clears away
the rust of the whole
week.

JOSEPH ADDISON

*S*how yourself in all
respects a model of
good deeds.

Keep one thing forever in view—the truth; and if you do this, though it may seem to lead you away from the opinion of men, it will assuredly conduct you to the throne of God.

✠ HORACE MANN ✠

The value of life lies not in the length of days, but in the use we make of them; a man may live long yet live very little.

✠ MONTAIGNE ✠

But there are seven sisters ever serving Truth,
Porters of the Posterns; one called Abstinence,
Humility, Charity, Chastity be the chief
maidens there;
Patience and Peace help many a one;
Lady Almsgiving lets in full many.

WILLIAM LANGLAND

No one may forsake his neighbor when he is in trouble. Everybody is under obligation to help and support his neighbor as he would himself like to be helped.

✝ MARTIN LUTHER ✝

200

Gradually I came to see that I could use the Bible, which had so baffled me, as an instrument for digging out precious truths, just as I could use my hindered, halting body for the high behests of my spirit.

HELEN KELLER

201

We have merely to assert what already exists deep within us—namely a sense of kinship.

✛ NORMAN COUSINS ✛

In proportion as we perceive and embrace the truth we do become just, heroic, magnanimous, divine.

WILLIAM LLOYD GARRISON

For a man to argue, "I do not go to church; I pray alone," is no wiser than if he should say, "I have no use for symphonies; I believe only in solo music."

✠ GEORGE A. BUTTRICK ✠

Christianity knows no truth which is not the child of love and the parent of duty.

PHILLIPS BROOKS

What you are is God's gift to you; what you make of it is your gift to God.

ANTHONY DALLA VILLA

Don't try to hold God's hand; let Him hold yours. Let Him do the holding, and you the trusting.

HAMMER WILLIAM WEBB-PEPLOE

How ready is heaven to those that pray!

BEN JONSON

The prayer that reforms the sinner and heals the sick is an absolute faith that all things are possible to God,—a spiritual understanding of Him, an unselfed love.

✠ MARY BAKER EDDY ✠

He is blessed over all mortals who loses no moment of the passing life in remembering the past.

HENRY DAVID THOREAU

210

To every thing there is a season, and a time to every purpose under the heaven.

ECCLESIASTES 3:1

We are born in relation, we live in relation, we die in relation. There is, literally, no such human place as simply "inside myself." Nor is any person, creed, ideology, or movement entirely "outside myself."

✢ CARTER HEYWARD ✢

But after that the kindness and love of God our Saviour toward man appeared, Not by works of righteousness which we have done, but according to his mercy he saved us, by the washing of regeneration, and renewing of the Holy Ghost.

TITUS 3:4–5

The deepest truth
blooms only from the
deepest love.

HEINRICH HEINE

Do not pray for easy lives. Pray to be stronger men.

JOHN F. KENNEDY

There is no heaven
like mutual love.

GEORGE GRANVILLE

216

There is no wealth
but life.

John Ruskin

Love, like the opening of the heavens to the saints, shows for a moment, even to the dullest man, the possibilities of the human race. He has faith, hope, and charity for another being, perhaps but the creation of his imagination; still it is a great advance for a man to be profoundly loving, even in his imagination.

✠ SIR ARTHUR HELPS ✠

Christianity is different from all other religions. They are the story of man's search for God. The Gospel is the story of God's search for man.

✠ DEWI MORGAN ✠

While faith makes all things possible, it is love that makes all things easy.

EVAN H. HOPKINS

Home is where the heart is.

ANONYMOUS

Two souls with but a
single thought,
Two hearts that beat as
one.

FRANZ JOSEPH
VON MÜNCH-BELLINGHAUSEN

If you do not hope,
you will not find what
is beyond your hopes.

ST. CLEMENT OF ALEXANDRIA

Instead of allowing yourself to be so unhappy, just let your love grow as God wants it to grow; seek goodness in others, love more persons more; love them more impersonally, more unselfishly, without thought of return. The return, never fear, will take care of itself.

HENRY DRUMMOND

For God hath not called us unto uncleanness, but unto holiness.

THESSALONIANS 4:7

True it is that marriages be done in heaven and performed on earth.

WILLIAM PAINTER

Death gives life its fullest reality.

ANTHONY DALLA VILLA

God loveth a cheerful giver.

II Corinthians 9:7

Love is the doorway through which the human soul passes from selfishness to service and from solitude to kinship with all mankind.

✠ ANONYMOUS ✠

Faith is to believe what you do not yet see; the reward for this faith is to see what you believe.

ST. AUGUSTINE

Christianity is the least concerned about religion of any of the world's faiths. It is primarily concerned about life.

✛ T. D. PRICE ✛

A true Christian should have but one fear—lest he should not hope enough.

WALTER ELLIOT

The true Christian is the true citizen, lofty of purpose, resolute in endeavor, ready for a hero's deeds, but never looking down on his task because it is cast in the day of small things; scornful of baseness, awake to his own duties as well as to his rights, following the higher law with reverence, and in this world doing all that in his power lies, so that when death comes he may feel that mankind is in some degree better because he lived.

THEODORE ROOSEVELT

The word which God has written on the brow of every man is Hope.

VICTOR HUGO

What is brotherhood?
Brotherhood is giving to others
the rights you want to keep for
yourself ... giving to the
individual in another group the
same dignity, the same full
appreciation that you want to
have yourself.

EVERETT R. CLINCHY

For the Lord is good; his mercy is everlasting; and his truth endureth to all generations.

✛ PSALMS 100:5 ✛

I do not pray for a lighter load, but for a stronger back.

PHILLIPS BROOKS

Thou shalt love thy neighbor as thyself.

LEVITICUS 19:18

The purpose of Christianity is not to avoid difficulty, but to produce a character adequate to meet it when it comes. It does not make life easy; rather it tries to make us great enough for life.

JAMES L. CHRISTENSEN

Every happening, great and small, is a parable whereby God speaks to us, and the art of life is to get the message.

✤ MALCOLM MUGGERIDGE ✤

The true way to be humble is not to stoop until you are smaller than yourself, but to stand at your real height against some higher nature that will show you what the real smallness of your greatness is.

PHILLIPS BROOKS

Until you know that life is interesting—and find it so—you haven't found your soul.

Christianity is the power of God in the soul of man.

ROBERT BOYD MUNGER

Hope is some extraordinary
spiritual grace that God gives us
to control our fears,
not to oust them.

✠ VINCENT MCNABB ✠

Happy is the house that shelters a friend!

RALPH WALDO EMERSON

Christianity is not a theory or speculation, but a life; not a philosophy of life, but a living presence.

✠ SAMUEL TAYLOR COLERIDGE ✠

And now abideth faith, hope, and charity, these three; but the greatest of these is charity.

✠ I CORINTHIANS 13:13 ✠

True humility is intelligent self-respect which keeps us from thinking too highly or too meanly of ourselves. It makes us mindful of the nobility God meant us to have. Yet it makes us modest by reminding us how far we have come short of what we can be.

RALPH W. SOCKMAN

No one is without Christianity, if we agree
on what we mean by the word. It is every
individual's individual code of behavior by
means of which he makes himself a better
human being than his nature wants to be,
if he followed his nature only.

WILLIAM FAULKNER

When we were watching the distribution of clothing in Jordan, I found myself wondering what it would be like to be wearing the clothes of someone else; how it would be like always in someone else's shoes. Then it occurred to me that this is precisely what Christianity means— eternally being in someone else's shoes.

R. PAUL FREED

Hunting God is a
great adventure.

MARIE DE FLORIS

And this I do believe above all, especially in times of greater discouragement, that I must believe—that I must believe in my fellow men—that I must believe in myself—that I must believe in God—if life is to have any meaning.

MARGARET CHASE SMITH

Jesus Christ is the same yesterday, and today, and forever.

HEBREWS 13:8

Away in foreign fields they wondered how
    Their simple words had power—
At home the Christians, two or three had met
    To pray an hour.
Yes, we are always wondering, wondering how—
    Because we do not see
Someone—perhaps unknown and far away—
    On bended knee.

ANONYMOUS

And he said to them all,
"If any man will come after me,
let him deny himself, and take up
his cross daily, and follow me."

✚ LUKE 9:23 ✚

We not only live among men, but there are airy hosts, blessed spectators, sympathetic lookers-on, that see and know and appreciate our thoughts and feelings and acts.

✠ HENRY WARD BEECHER ✠

What enthusiasm is to the youth and ambition to the apprentice and peace of mind to the invalid, such is hope to the Christians.

✠ JOSEPH MCSORLEY ✠

Respect is what we owe; love, what we give.

PHILIP JAMES BAILEY

True Love is but a humble, low-born thing,
And hath its food served up in earthen ware;
It is a thing to walk with, hand in hand,
Through the everydayness of this
workday world.

JAMES RUSSELL LOWELL

Love is the only
service that power
cannot command and
money cannot buy.

ANONYMOUS

Hospitality
consists in a little fire,
a little food, and an
immense quiet.

RALPH WALDO EMERSON

We never know how much one loves till we know how much he is willing to endure and suffer for us; and it is the suffering element that measures love. The characters that are great must, of necessity, be characters that shall be willing, patient and strong to endure for others. To hold our nature in the willing service of another, is the divine idea of manhood, of the human character.

HENRY WARD BEECHER

And Jesus answered him, saying, "It is written that 'Man shall not live by bread alone, but by every word of God.'"

✠ LUKE 4:4 ✠

The cure for all the ills and wrongs, the cares, the sorrows, and the crimes of humanity, all lie in that one word "love." It is the divine vitality that everywhere produces and restores life. To each and every one of us, it gives the power of working miracles if we will.

LYDIA MARIA CHILD

The most disadvantageous peace is better than the most just war.

DESIDERIUS ERASMUS

Trust begets truth.

SIR WILLIAM GURNEY BENHAM

The glory of Christianity is to conquer by forgiveness.

WILLIAM BLAKE

The best repentance is to get up and act for righteousness, and forget that you ever had relations with sin.

✠ WILLIAM JAMES ✠

It is right to hate sin,
but not to hate the
sinner.

GIOVANNI GUARESCHI

As it obliged him to respect the presence of God in others, so it obliged him to respect the presence of God in himself, to make himself the messenger of God, or the path taken by God.

✠ ANTOINE DE SAINT-EXUPÉRY ✠

The pure soul
Shall mount on native wings,
disdaining little sport,
And cut a path into the heaven of glory,
Leaving a track of light for men to wonder at.

WILLIAM BLAKE

Serve the Lord with gladness: come before his presence with singing.

PSALMS 100:2

The body is the
soul's image; therefore
keep it pure.

POPE XYSTUS I

All that is necessary to salvation is contained in two virtues: faith in Christ, and obedience to laws.

✛ THOMAS HOBBES ✛

No one can ask honestly or happily to be delivered from temptation unless he has honestly and firmly determined to do the best he can to keep out of it.

✠ JOHN RUSKIN ✠

Let us, like [Mary], touch the dying, the poor, the lonely and the unwanted according to the graces we have received and let us not be ashamed or slow to do the humble work.

✠ MOTHER TERESA ✠

Every time you pray, if your prayer is sincere, there will be new feeling and new meaning in it which will give you fresh courage, and you will understand that prayer is an education.

FYODOR DOSTOYEVSKY

To love truth is the principal part of human perfection in this world, and the seed-plot of all other virtues.

✣ JOHN LOCKE ✣

One should believe
in marriage as in the
immortality of the
soul.

HONORÉ DE BALZAC

Some trust in chariots, and some in horses: but we will remember the name of the Lord our God.

✤ PSALMS 20:7 ✤

Perfection consists not in doing extraordinary things, but in doing ordinary things extraordinarily well. Neglect nothing; the most trivial action may be performed to God.

✠ ANGÉLIQUE ARNAULD ✠

Let us no more contend, nor blame
Each other, blam'd enough elsewhere, but strive
In offices of love, how we may lighten
Each other's burden, in our share of woe.

JOHN MILTON

We arrive at truth,
not by reason only,
but also by the heart.

PASCAL

The Cross does not abolish suffering, but transforms it, sanctifies it, makes it fruitful, bearable, even joyful, and finally victorious.

✠ JOSEPH RICKABY ✠

The most eloquent prayer is the prayer through hands that heal and bless. The highest form of worship is the worship of unselfish Christian service. The greatest form of praise is the sound of consecrated feet seeking out the lost and helpless.

BILLY GRAHAM

The simple heart
that freely asks in love,
obtains.

JOHN GREENLEAF WHITTIER

The grace of God is in my mind shaped like a key, that comes from time to time and unlocks the heavy doors.

✠ DONALD SWAN ✠

The Christian religion, by confining marriage to pairs, and rendering the relation indissoluble, has by these two things done more toward the peace, happiness, settlement, and civilization of the world, than by any other part in this whole scheme of divine wisdom.

EDMUND BURKE

Self-discipline never means
giving up anything—for giving up is a loss.
Our Lord did not ask us to give up the things
of earth, but to exchange them for better things.

BISHOP FULTON J. SHEEN

Religion without joy—it is no religion.

THEODORE PARKER

The ever-living Christ is here to bless you. The nearer you keep him, the nearer you will be to one another.

GEOFFREY FISHER
ARCHBISHOP OF CANTERBURY

Judge not, and ye shall not be judged: condemn not, and ye shall not be condemned: forgive, and ye shall be forgiven.

✢ LUKE 6:37 ✢

For every creature of God is good, and nothing to be refused, if it be received with thanksgiving: For it is sanctified by the word of God and prayer.

✛ I TIMOTHY 4:4–5 ✛

To be human is to be
challenged to be more divine.
Not even to try to meet such a
challenge is the biggest defeat
imaginable.

✟ MAYA ANGELOU ✟

True piety hath in it nothing weak, nothing sad, nothing constrained. It enlarges the heart; it is simple, free, and attractive.

✠

FRANÇOIS DE SALIGNAC
DE LA MOTHE FÉNELON

And though I have the gift of prophecy, and understand all mysteries, and all knowledge; and though I have all faith, so that I could remove mountains, and have not charity, I am nothing.

I CORINTHIANS 13:2

He who stops being better stops being good.

OLIVER CROMWELL

Love is an act of
endless forgiveness, a
tender look which
becomes a habit.

PETER USTINOV

Prayer is the soul's sincere desire,
    Uttered or unexpressed,
The motion of a hidden fire
    That trembles in the breast.

Prayer is the burden of a sigh,
    The falling of a tear,
The upward glancing of an eye
    When none but God is near.

JAMES MONTGOMERY

The important thing
is to begin again,
humbly and
courageously, after
every fall.

✠ DOM HELDER CAMARA ✠

Prayer is love raised to its greatest power, and the prayer of intercession is the noblest and most Christian kind of prayer because in it love—and imagination—reach their highest and widest range.

ROBERT J. McCRACKEN

Religion is not an intelligence test, but a faith.

EDGAR WATSON HOWE

Trouble and perplexity drive
me to prayer, and prayer drives
away perplexity and trouble.

✤ PHILIP MELANCHTHON ✤

A man that hath friends must show himself friendly: and there is a friend that sticketh closer than a brother.

✠ PROVERBS 18:24 ✠

We ought to act with God in the greatest simplicity, speaking to Him frankly and plainly, and imploring His assistance in our affairs, just as they happen.

✠ BROTHER LAWRENCE ✠

Blessed is the man that endureth temptation.

JAMES 1:12

Prayer is not conquering God's reluctance, but taking hold of God's willingness.

✠ PHILLIPS BROOKS ✠

No man has the
right to abandon the
care of his salvation to
another.

THOMAS JEFFERSON

Prayer is and remains
always a native and
deepest impulse of the
soul of man.

✝ THOMAS CARLYLE ✝

When all our efforts have come to nothing,
we naturally tend to doubt not just ourselves,
but also whether God is just. At those
moments, our only hope is to seek every
evidence that God *is* just, by communing
with the people we know who are
strongest in their faith.

BILL MOYERS

Prayer is the most powerful form of energy one can generate. The influence of prayer on the human mind and body is as demonstrable as that of the secreting glands. Prayer is a force as real as terrestrial gravity. It supplies us with a flow of sustaining power in our daily lives.

ALEXIS CARREL

Throughout this varied and eternal world Soul is the only element.

PERCY BYSSHE SHELLEY

Prayer is exhaling the spirit of man and inhaling the spirit of God.

EDWIN KEITH

Pray without ceasing.

I Thessalonians 5:17

Stay, stay at home, my heart, and rest;
Home-keeping hearts are happiest,
For those that wander they know not where
Are full of trouble and full of care;
To stay at home is best.

HENRY WADSWORTH LONGFELLOW

Give to the world
the best you have and
the best will come
back to you.

ANONYMOUS

Speak, move, act in peace, as if you were in prayer. In truth, this is prayer.

FRANÇOIS DE SALIGNAC
DE LA MOTHE FÉNELON

317

Belief is a truth held in the mind; faith is a fire in the heart.

JOSEPH FORT NEWTON

My country is the world, and my religion is to do good.

Thomas Paine

Fear knocked at the door. Faith answered. No one was there.

INSCRIPTION AT HIND'S HEAD INN,

BRAY, ENGLAND

Faith is the sense of life, that sense by virtue of which man does not destroy himself, but continues to live on. It is the force whereby we live.

✠ LEO TOLSTOY ✠

For God hath not given us the spirit of fear; but of power, and of love, and of a sound mind.

✠ II TIMOTHY 1:7 ✠

What shall it profit a man, if he shall gain the whole world, and lose his own soul?

✠ MARK 8:36 ✠

Christianity is the science of character building, the philosophy of immortality, the logic of earth and heaven contacts, the solution of the riddle of existence.

✝ ANONYMOUS ✝

The Christian is not one who has gone all the way with Christ. None of us has. The Christian is one who has found the right road.

✠ CHARLES L. ALLEN ✠

The Lord is on my side; I will not fear: what can man do unto me?

PSALMS 118:6

Let the Divine Mind flow through your own mind, and you will be happier. I have found the greatest power in the world in the power of prayer. There is no shadow of doubt of that. I speak from my own experience.

CECIL B. DEMILLE

Live and let live.

SCOTTISH PROVERB

The goal of the Christian life is not to save your soul but to transcend yourself, to vindicate the human struggle of which all of us are a part, to keep hope advancing.

WILLIAM SLOANE COFFIN, JR.

Religion itself is nothing else but Love to God and man.

WILLIAM PENN

The soul of the
Christian religion is
reverence.

J. W. VON GOETHE

Therefore if any man be in Christ, he is a new creature: old things are passed away; behold, all things are become new.

✠ II CORINTHIANS 5:17 ✠

The Christians do not commit adultery. They do not bear false witness. They do not covet their neighbor's goods. They honor father and mother. They love their neighbors. They judge justly. They avoid doing to others what they do not wish done to them. They do good to their enemies. They are kind.

St. Aristides

The wealth of the soul is the only true wealth.

LUCIAN

Love, which is the essence of God, is not for levity, but for the total worth of man.

✤ RALPH WALDO EMERSON ✤

Every Christian truth,
gracious and comfortable,
has a corresponding obligation,
searching and sacrificial.

✜ HARRY EMERSON FOSDICK ✜

In this world it is not what we take up, but what we give up, that makes us rich.

HENRY WARD BEECHER

If you wish your children to be Christians you must really take the trouble to be Christian yourselves. Those are the only terms upon which the home will work the gracious miracle.

WOODROW WILSON

K

now ye not that ye are the
temple of God, and that the
Spirit of God dwelleth in you?

✝ I CORINTHIANS 3:16 ✝

The truth shall make you free.

JOHN 8:32

God helps those that help themselves.

BENJAMIN FRANKLIN

He that sees the beauty of holiness, or true moral good, sees the greatest and most important thing in the world ... There is no other true excellence or beauty.

JONATHAN EDWARDS

Religion is more like response to a friend than it is like obedience to an expert.

AUSTIN FARRER

Happy is the man
that findeth wisdom,
and the man that
getteth understanding.

PROVERBS 3:13

Giving is the secret of a healthy life. Not necessarily money, but whatever a man has of encouragement and sympathy and understanding.

✠ JOHN D. ROCKEFELLER, JR. ✠

They that sow in tears shall reap in joy.

P<small>SALMS</small> 126:5

By friendship you mean the greatest love, the greatest usefulness, the most open communication, the noblest sufferings, the severest truth, the heartiest counsel, and the greatest union of minds of which brave men and women are capable.

JEREMY TAYLOR

The first and last lesson of religion is, "The things that are seen are temporal; the things that are unseen are eternal."
It puts an affront upon nature.

✠ RALPH WALDO EMERSON ✠

Blessed are the poor in spirit: for theirs is
   the kingdom of heaven.
Blessed are they that mourn: for they shall be
   comforted.
Blessed are the meek: for they shall inherit the
   earth.
Blessed are they which do hunger and thirst after
   righteousness: for they shall be filled.
Blessed are the merciful: for they shall obtain mercy.
Blessed are the pure in heart: for they shall see God.
Blessed are the peacemakers: for they shall be called
   the children of God.
Blessed are they which are persecuted for righteous-
   ness sake: for theirs is the kingdom of heaven.

✙ MATTHEW 5:3–10 ✙

Good to forget—
Best to forgive!

ROBERT BROWNING

Belief consists in accepting
the affirmations of the soul;
unbelief, in denying them.

✠ RALPH WALDO EMERSON ✠

There are no
miracles to men who
do not believe in
them.

ANONYMOUS

No man is a true Christian who does not think constantly of how he can lift his brother, how he can assist his friend, how he can enlighten mankind, how he can make virtue the rule of conduct in the circle in which he lives.

WOODROW WILSON

We love him, because he first loved us.

I JOHN 4:19

Faith is the heart of the mind.

ANONYMOUS

Now I lay me down to sleep;
I pray the Lord my soul to keep.
If I should die before I wake,
I pray the Lord my soul to take.

✟ ANONYMOUS ✟

Entirely by yourself as an individual you can go to hell, but alone you cannot go to heaven, for to go to heaven we need what one may call the natural grace of the mutual dependence on each other here on earth.

FRANCIS DEVAS

Faith is the daring of
the soul to go farther
than it can see.

WILLIAM NEWTON CLARKE

Ail the kindness which a man
puts out into the world works on
the heart and thoughts of
mankind.

✠ ALBERT SCHWEITZER ✠

True repentance is to cease from sin.

ST. AMBROSE

I̲t is more blessed to give than to receive.

ACTS 20:35

The enduring value of religion is in its challenge to aspiration and hope in the mind of man.

✠ ERNEST MARTIN HOPKINS ✠

Kindness has converted more people than zeal, science, or eloquence.

MOTHER TERESA

Give plenty of
what is given to you,
And listen to pity's call;
Don't think the little
you give is great
And the much you
get is small.

✠ PHOEBE CARY ✠

Religious faith is not a storm cellar to which men and women can flee for refuge from the storms of life. It is, instead, an inner spiritual strength which enables them to face those storms with hope and serenity. Religious faith has the miraculous power to lift ordinary human beings to greatness in seasons of stress.

✟ SAM J. ERVIN, JR. ✟

My son, keep your spirit always in such a state as to desire that there be a God, and you will never doubt it.

✠ JEAN JACQUES ROUSSEAU ✠

Never lose
a chance of saying
a kind word.

WILLIAM MAKEPEACE THACKERAY

He loves each one of us,
as if there were only
one of us.

✠ ST. AUGUSTINE ✠

Let love be your greatest aim.

1 Corinthians 14:1

To forgive is the highest, most beautiful form of love. In return, you will receive untold peace and happiness.

✢ ROBERT MULLER ✢

God's love elevates
us without inflating us,
and humbles us without
degrading us.

B. NOTTAGE

We have within ourselves
Enough to fill the present day
with joy, And overspread the
future years with hope.

✠ WILLIAM WORDSWORTH ✠

Never forget to be truthful and kind. Hold these virtues tightly. Write them deep within your heart.

✤ PROVERBS 3:3–4 ✤

The text of this book was set in Centaur,

Charlemagne, and Evangel

by Harry Chester Inc.

Book design by

Judith Stagnitto Abbate